THE POET'S POCKET GUIDE TO STEADY EMPLOYMENT

Poems
Bill Van Buskirk

The Poet's Pocket Guide
to Steady Employment
by

Bill Van Buskirk

All words contained herein are © 2023 by Bill Van Buskirk.

No part of this book may be reproduced in any form without the express written permission of the author. The sole exception to this prohibition would be in the case of brief quotations embodied in critical articles or reviews, and pages where permission is specifically granted by the publisher or author.
Some parts of this work have appeared in slightly different form in periodicals and books prior to the publication of this volume:

Comstock Review: Ice King; The Poet at 70.
Journal of Management Education: Sensei.
Mad Poet's Review: Alchemy 101.
Parting Gifts: The Poet's Pocket Guide to Steady Employment; Pop; All Souls; Matthew Gandalf.
Paterson Literary Review: My Father and Jesus, At the AT&T Stockholder's Meeting, October 31, 1970.
Philadelphia Poets: Ice Age; Tyger, Tyger; Akhmatova's Triumph; Autobiography of a Stranger; Confidence; A Postcard to My Mother Two Weeks After Her Death.

Published by Parnilis Media
PO Box 1461,
Media, Pennsylvania, 19063

Printed in the United States of America

PHILADELPHIA POETS RESPOND TO THE WORK OF BILL VAN BUSKIRK

"A poet should be useful," says Bill Van Buskirk in the title poem of *The Poet's Pocket Guide to Steady Employment*. He achieves much with these poems, which startle and deeply affect their reader. This collection rouses us and invites us in while also challenging us with complex layers and fresh ideas. Van Buskirk's language is precise, economical, and original ("fateful dash of sperm to egg") as he writes on topics from the personal to the cultural—always with the poet's clear, sharp eye at the center. *Pocket Guide* may not steer you to a good job, but it will take you on a ride that has you looking forward to each new discovery, each bounce and curve.

Abbey Porter.

The Poet's Pocket Guide to Steady Employment could more honestly be called *The Reader's Guide to Steady Enjoyment*. This little volume provides a gateway to something beyond the mundane to the magical. The reader is bidden to... "Present yourself to all that you are not. It will shape you." Certainly, there is some angst and agony. There is even death. But the author of the *Poet's Guide* does not leave even the dead for dead. There is an underlying humor, sly understatement, knowing resignation, and redemption. At its core, empathic and companionable, Bill's verse shines with the same twinkle that animates his eyes when he performs his work, a light that complements the noir tinge of the verse. You'll find *The Poet's Guide to Steady Employment* good reading and good company. May the Guide be with you!

Michael Cohen.

Misery and miracles, sinners and angels cruising in for soft landings in our parlors mingle in Bill Van Buskirk's newest collection of poems. His writing completely refreshes: "the first snowflakes—not much more than thickened air themselves—just beginning to fall." He wonders about everything gigantic in the universe at the same time he notices the light on a lemon in the passing afternoon. Read this book and take his advice: Be the vast welter of yourself— its contradiction, its magnificence. If your guts squirm like snakes in a pit, if your stories tie themselves in knots, let them.

Amy Laub,
author of What water says (2021) and
There is no cure for this: Ocean & moon poems (2022)

Bill Van Buskirk has created a book of poems you must read! Edgy, coarse and beautiful. In their presence, you cannot help being changed by the language, the emotional impact.

Ed Krizek.

I have known Bill for over twenty-eight years and have read and heard these beloved poems many times. They have a way of being both fresh and new and yet deeply familiar. There is a sense of the divine in all his characters as they show us their complex and often messy humanity; and once they find their way into your soul, you will never let them go.

Lisa De Vuono.

Great poems stay with you long after you have read them. In *The Poet's Pocket Guide to Steady Employment*, Bill Van Buskirk's new collection, his poems certainly do that. I ask myself, "How does he do it?" But the question quickly fades because I can't get the last poem out of my head. I turn the page, read on. The same thing happens, and it continues through all 39 poems. I search for something to say that can accurately convey how good this book is. Wouldn't you know, I found it in Bill's on words from the poem, Alchemy 101—"This is the nub of great magic." Yes, it is!

Steve Delia.

Move over Wallace Stevens. Bill Van Buskirk is taking your parking space.

Robert Kramer,
Budapest, Hungary.

Praise for This Wild Joy that Thrills Outside the Law

The collection tackles some of life's biggest, most persistent questions (of truth and lies, of love and war) in pieces that are compact, unassuming, and humble. Truman Capote has said that "The problem with living outside the law is that you no longer have its protection." *This Wild Joy that Thrills Outside the Law* seeks not to protect, but to reveal. The collection is wild, thrilling, and full of joy. Both taunting and embracing the limits and limitations of time, the collection yields gifts of snow days, winter stews, and culinary feasts. Of fathers and fate. Of coffee and foggy mornings. Of lineage and strong women. Of common discourse and contemplative conversation. With language, style, and tone that are both understated and remarkable, the work is written of and for anyone with a curiosity for life. For living. It's for those who live and have lived. It's for anyone eager to explore life surprises - both in and outside the law.

Jen Schneider

Dedication

This book is dedicated to the members of the Wild Surmise Poetry Circle without whose generous feedback it never would have been written: Frank Barrett, Elizabeth Baron, Lisa Baron, Kathy Bishop, Mary Croke, Rachel Ellsworth, Carol Gray, Phyllis Greenwald, John Hickey, Kathy Kane, Robert Kramer, Michael London, Kathy McMearty, Jacob Sheetz-Willard, Woody Sheetz-Willard, Jim Stoner, Judy Van Buskirk

CONTENTS

MUSE	3
SINGING LESSON	4
HIGH COMEDY	6
POP	8
THE POET'S POCKET GUIDE TO STEADY EMPLOYMENT	10
MEDIA	11
ALI RENOUNCES THE SLAVE NAME	12
GRANDFATHER'S ADVICE	14
ALCHEMY 101	16
ICE KING	17
ICE AGE	18
MY FATHER AND JESUS	20
POSTCARD TO MY MOTHER: TWO YEARS AFTER HER DEATH	22
VOICE	23
ALL SOULS	24
LAZARUS ON HIS SECOND DEATHBED REMEMBERS	25
BLOOD	26
MATTHEW GANDALF	27
VALEDICTORY	28
OPENING NIGHT	30
THE POET AT 70	32
ANTHEM	33
AUTOBIOGRAPHY OF A STRANGER	34
Jesus is my religion and pool is my game	36
GRANDAD'S TRIP	37
AKHMATOVA'S TRIUMPH	38
SENSEI	40
ODE TO THE ORDER	42
NUNS	44
TYGER, TYGER	45
UNDERWORLD	46
GRANDFATHER PLAYS CHESS WITH DEATH AT THE AT&T STOCKHOLDER MEETING, OCTOBER 31, 1970	48 / 49
CONFIDENCE	50
WHY I DON'T MARCH ON THE 4TH OF JULY	52
NAMING DAY	54
SURF MUSIC	56
MUSE AT THE WEDDING	58
BIOGRAPHY	60

MUSE
(For K.B.)

The bar was a bad habit.
It smelled of everything that ever happened there—
tobacco, marijuana, and a thousand nights
of spilled beer.

She caught my eye.
The evening sparkled.

But she was surrounded by musicians
with hooded eyes and ulterior motives.

My eyes were mirrors.
Hers were moons.
I couldn't tell what color they were.

I wondered could she see
through the haze of smoke and strobe
how she lit up the room
for me.

I wasn't optimistic.
For an hour or so I took her in
with a patient gaze.

Then she made her move—
a beer in each hand—

"Tell me what you love," she said.
"Tell me all about it."

SINGING LESSON

To learn the hymn of praise start anywhere—
fateful dash of sperm to egg, congenial womb,
father on the train each morning
as you take shape in bliss...

    Perhaps you feel it—

this trembling web, this good thick tapestry tangling
inside you and out.

    Praise it. Praise every tender thread that makes
    you up.

Praise the brain, the nerves, the yards and yards of guts.
Praise the veins, arteries, alleyways, boulevards,
highways,
and don't forget the gene—destiny encoded
in the slenderest threads encircling the globe
to bring us—coffee beans from Brazil,
yogurt from good Pennsylvania cows,
bananas, the evening fish and rice, and you
at its center—suspended in the weave—

thickening into being all at once...

  Praise it all. Praise

this fragile, blazing world we make—
so different from the old one—
dead objects divorced
from one another and from you.

    Why do you stay there—

where the ocean that you bob on
is mistaken for a big idea?

    Come, join us—the eight billion

who suck at the teats of the universe!
Half-formed, much beloved, we hang helpless in
bunches—
grapes, apples, peaches—ripening, connected
even when our time is almost up
like patients hooked to their last I.V.'s—
some still hum a little tune—
stalk, throat, placenta, bloom…

HIGH COMEDY

Convivo ergo sum. I party, therefore I am.
                                    James Hillman

Once again last Saturday
we laughed so hard that tears
streamed down our faces. We wept
in the quaking carnival of all we were
'til even our bones were funny—
skeletons tingling to the same jingles.

Too much wine
was certainly part of it. Now we look back
in wonder, try to remember labels
on the bottles. We long for that trance
to be our sun and moon, to wear bright red
pajamas and cakewalk on the boulevard.

I search for a sober word to hold all this
but it can't say how our hearts spilled out
onto the sidewalk, set up shop for an evening,
rattled their tin cups at random passersby

or how we reveled until three AM
in a world too vast for old ways of being new,

or how our dreams dressed up themselves
in ancient images: new ways
of being old—*wrinkled, antic*—

we don't explain. We greet
whoever shows up in our days, especially
the young suicides. The work is urgent—
this search for

songs,
        jokes,
                slivers of shtick

strong enough to sweep them up in our gaiety…

Join us! Join us! We say.
We know a better way to die.

POP

-1-

I was a kid—alone,
surrounded by voices
that grownups couldn't hear—
giving bad advice
like the Church that said

you are sinful, breathe
as infrequently as possible.

So you see, I was desperate
for a second opinion on spiritual matters.

Pop never talked about gods,
but he *had* worked in the textile mills,
got by on disability, and so had time
for some opinions of his own.

Already out of favor
in the year I was born,
he lived in sin with Irene
between the river and the railroad tracks.
But what he left us was enough for me--
a happy memory of who he was,
a sly echo of a life of song and dance
that plays on where grownups cannot go.

But he was a little too lively to be safe,
so we never got to see him except
on Christmas and Easter
when he was grateful.

-2-

Anyhow, that's why, years later,
I didn't run away when
we played spin-the-bottle
at Wendy's mother's house—
my future close enough
to smell the perfume, that bottle
in slow motion like a dream—
spin and tip, toward, away

from who I'd get to kiss—
that pulse in my neck going crazy

like now—

when there's too much money down
and the wheel spins, dice tumble,
the last card snaps and the thrill
of soon-but-not-yet
slips through the thicket
of your sins—

like this flirtation with all that's next,

that shows how risk and joy
can propel a life

like a law of physics—

juxtaposition

      explosion

            momentum

and where you end up—
here, trembling.

THE POET'S POCKET GUIDE TO STEADY EMPLOYMENT

A poet should be useful—like a stoneworker—
bright eyed in the ruins, re-building the Cathedral of Silence
with the words of his time for bricks: like Chartres—all that

solid masonry—quarried, dragged and cut—to hold
a hush, an atmosphere, a shiver from nowhere, a dove in the rafters.
So, be useful. Conjure, rhapsodize, savor, make it real—that
holy moment—

when you choose Poverty and accumulate Ease,
choose Obscurity and know Fame for what it is—
a pretty good idea that needs a lot of work.

Why, someday you might hit it big—
do something truly useful like trick a bit
of movement from an old sin that's put down

roots in our blur of buy-and-sell, or accidentally
name a new one metastasizing somewhere
between boredom and despair.

I mean, *somebody* has to do it.
These recently implanted lusts
just have to be identified and categorized

like a new species—a dark mushroom maybe—

waiting to be tasted.

MEDIA

I heard that Terri Gross is a tiny little thing,
but her voice is big—tender, generous, fearless.

I know a guy in California who wants
to marry her, wants to hear her

all day long, all night too—twenty-four seven.
I can't blame him. The Golden Age of Radio

had a lot of soul in it. Spirited voices brought the news
in tones that heroes spoke or maybe angels cruising

in for soft landings in our parlors—
giving us time to ponder things—

not like now—when the power-mad
try to do our thinking for us, cram us

with their images, innuendoes and irresistible offers—
like that one I heard today—this company wants

to take my pulse twenty-four-seven
and feed it to its data base.

What will become of us? we think,
as we rush past one another in the street.

Terri isn't bothered by all this.
She knows the untapped power

in the flick of a toggle…
                    on, off…on, off.

ALI RENOUNCES THE SLAVE NAME

The hand can't hit
What the eye don't see
Float like a butterfly, sting like a bee.
Rumble young man, rumble!
                    Mohammad Ali

Free at last! Free at last!
Thank God Almighty I'm free at last.

                    Martin Luther king

...so he steps up
to the rippling bulk
of Liston or Foreman,
oiled in the lights
and sniffs,
brazens his stare
into the molten danger.

How deep does it go?

No matter.

For he knows now
what you're called is

how you think and what you do.

He has found the punch
in his talk, renounced the master—
his name, his thoughts without poetry—
renounced the old sad songs
his people sang themselves
to sleep with.

He thinks:
Suffering is endless
Desire…endless.

At the bell
his dance is also endless.

His fate broods
in a dark body
that cannot comprehend him.
He flicks a jab
at it

watches it wince and hunkerdown.

He learns

something of its movement—
shuffles, feints, leans
away from a lethal right,
orbits
the dense stare
of muscle—

like a doomed moon
and it's dark star.

No matter,
for he's too busy burning.

He knows now how it feels
at last
when breath flares into myth
at last, at last.

GRANDFATHER'S ADVICE

Beware the language of slaves.

It is spoken everywhere—

welter of prohibition,
peevish command,
muttered grunt of deference,
sacred vow of retribution—

do not traffic in these
or hold them to your breast,
for they are like scorpions
stinging over and over.
For a lifetime
they will fester in your body
like spoiled meat.

Wonder, marvel, savor, mourn--
these strange verbs, these renegades
will befriend you in tight places.

Others have gone before.
They have seeded the language
with treasure—molten ruby, frosted jade.
If you find it, it will wake you up
and something small will change
in a thousand years of talk.

Behold your inheritance—

this thundering Amazon,
anonymous and wild,
muscling its way toward
something deep and blind.

Dive! Dive! Down through winter seas.

Forsake the sun!
Escape the sorcerer moon!

Slither deep! Grow gills!
Trust volcanoes bubbling in the seabed.

Make new friends.

ALCHEMY 101

Let yourself be tutored by your moments—
itch after itch, wince after wince, inkling after inkling.
Let true power come to know itself.

Sooner or later something sparks, flares, feeds
on what has gone before, until even the mountain
burns. There is no need whatsoever

to struggle. Present yourself to all
you know and trust. One thing will lead
to another. Be the vast welter of yourself—

its contradiction, its magnificence. If your guts
squirm like snakes in a pit, if your stories tie
themselves in knots, let them. If you are lost, then

you are lost. Don't hunker down
into a biography. Present yourself to all that you are not.
It will shape you.

    This is the nub of great magic.

So turn your gaze outward. Let the world's dance
become your own—the deep mathematic
of a symphony, maybe, or the light on a lemon

in the passing afternoon. This is amazing—
to know the night sky at the back
of your mind ever deepening into its rest

and how like a little spark in it you are.

ICE KING

It has snowed all day and it is snowing now
>at midnight. I've been digging out for hours –
>>no moon, no streetnoise, just me alone
>>>in the ghostly phosphorescence of the storm.

A massive swirl of white rises in the street
>and I think of my father and how he stood
>>on nights like this, one arm casually propped
>>>against the shovel, sure of his pacing and his strength—

I sniff ice crystals in like he did,
>mucus freezes, melts inside my nose. He says:
>>*But that's what the winter's for…so you can deepen into it.*
>>But I miss the thing that held him up —

confidence, a stake in the moment, supple vigor…
>him carried off before his time, me learning
>>the wrong lessons—to freeze too deep and call it safety—
>>>to be a stance without a story, a pose without a pulse in it.

Listen, he says, *my life was a song without an echo—mute*
>*unready to be sung. You'll know it by the rising heat,*
>>*wild and unbidden like a sun or my unspoken love.*
>>>*It is not for you to say when life is over. Live it*

like an epic with the end in sight:
>*crammed with contradiction,*
>>*too much wine,*
>>>*and with a death in it.*

ICE AGE

My father said—
   useful things are best.
He said—*the world is cold*

and snow began to fall day and night,
   undulant, silent, thick
enough to sleep in.

At school everyone agreed
   about use and winter
and how we should all keep busy.

I nodded solemnly—
   that snow
falling faster than any lesson,

memories snowbound,
   the sharp figures of my thinking
seized-up, frozen

from the inside out.
   In my twenties
I cried out to the sun god in a dream

and a wife came and then a lover
   and then more lovers and another wife
and then my brows turned white.

The world is cold, he said.
   It was his gift to me—the lesson
his life added up to.

Now I have my wish.
   The snows have stopped.
I stand amazed on the melting crust

of all that they have made,
eager for what else there is to do
in this, the only world I know—

the one that's been given,
the one that I must love.

MY FATHER AND JESUS

    1.

He was awake
when I arrived
at the hospital.
He wanted to talk
about Jesus.
I'd never seen him
so animated.
It was sort of
embarrassing.
He wanted to confide
how Jesus walked
with him every step
of a difficult life
and he never even knew it.
A part of me was
ironic and cruel—
    Irish Catholic deathbed—
it sneered.
I struggled to listen
but couldn't change
fast enough,
stuck in unfinished rebellions,
hating what I loved,
mute
in a body
long ago grown numb
to him…

2.

Twenty years later
I still search
for a way to bless him,
a way to enter
his inner world at the end—

a place to breathe
even as the body
slows and cools—

spirit going up in smoke
flesh collapsing into ash—

a flare so bright and sweet
it could have only seemed
a garden—wild with scent,
bright as fireworks
in a moonless Fourth of July—
full blooms of high summer—
hydrangea, zinnia, rose.

In *this* place
lungs are not the only things that breathe,
heart not the only thing that pulses.

In this place
I turn to him,
call him by his name
in all its fullness—
William, Harold, Father, Thou—
and conjure him a world
so bright and warm
he never even notices
how still he has become.

A POSTCARD TO MY MOTHER: TWO WEEKS AFTER HER DEATH

(For the Dharma Moon Sangha and the Mad Poets Society)

Remember when the tour guide said
how Melville read all plays of Shakespeare
in a single snowbound winter?

Well, that's the kind of company
I need now—sovereigns from the underworld
returned at last to greet me with the news

that I too might change utterly into something
lucky and relentless, muscling up in flesh and breath
even as the body slows, cools, becomes suffused
in pain a little more each year.

I have no parent now.

I seek new kin with strangers
who fall in love with whatever it is they do,
who find reflections in shadows cast by moons,
who thicken the air in broad daylight,
who have begun to taste their lives—

beginnings, endings—
like Melville opening Shakespeare by the lantern—
the first snowflakes— not much more
than thickened air themselves—

just beginning to fall.

VOICE

Where the voice that is in us makes a true response,
Where the voice that is great within us rises up...
   Wallace Stevens
   "Evening Without Angels."

It was five minutes 'til midnight at the crisis center. The phones were quiet. Our shift was almost up. Kay, Jimmie and me were the only ones left. It was my turn to clean up—mostly scraps of donut and styrofoam. The phone rang. Jimmie picked it up. I knew from his eyes that we were in trouble. It's for you, he said. I took the phone. It was Charlene from the therapy group. *I just called to hear your voice,* she said. She sounded vague, a little slurred. *I feel funny,* she said. FUNNY? I said. *Yeah. I wanted to die so I took some pills.* WHAT DID YOU TAKE? She recited the colors—*red, blue, green...*lucky for us Kay was a nurse. HOW MANY? *Oh, I dunno. Twenty, maybe thirty. I drank some booze too.* I said all this to Kay. THAT'S ENOUGH TO KILL HER, Kay said. Charlene's voice was fading. She hummed a little tune. WHERE ARE YOU? *In a phone booth.* WHERE? *Oh, I dunno. I love to hear your voice.* WHERE IS THE PHONE BOOTH? *That's a funny question. Who cares about where a phone booth is...*I mustered up as much force as I could. WHERE? *In the flats, by the river.* WHERE? *Oh I just love the sound of your voice.* TELL ME WHERE YOU ARE EXACTLY. *I don't want to.* WHY NOT? *The police will come. They'll take me to the hospital, make me throw up.* I froze. I wasn't ready. *I just wanna hear your voice.* What happened next...I still don't understand. It was like my brain stopped trying to stay afloat and something reckless, raw and angry took me over—It cut right through me and into her. ALL RIGHT, it said, SO YOU WANT ME TO TALK TO YOU WHILE YOU DIE. ALL RIGHT, I'LL DO THAT. WHAT DO YOU WANT TO TALK ABOUT? *Third and Carnegie!,* she said. *I'm in a phone booth at Third and Carnegie!* Anyhow, it worked out all right. Two years later she called from Minneapolis to say she'd had a kid.

ALL SOULS

Yesterday I gave up on words—
drank black coffee in Starbucks
content to see what happens in a Nothing
made of now, body and a little bit of rain
thickening into sleet
and an overnight howler
of a snowstorm big enough
to drift inside of—wind almost alive
in swirls of silver-dollar flakes
then, blasted apart.

They are like my thoughts.
Today, drinking coffee again,
I think of the dead trying so hard
to look like something familiar—
massive shrouds of white
not quite adding up
to an incarnation,
trying to capture—what?
A bit of attention maybe
now that daily street-noise
is muffled in the storm.

Now I'm not one
to mistake the drifting snow
for the love of God
or a lost parent,
but I am touched
when one of them,
lashed by a gale,
throws its unmade body
at the window where I sit and breaks
against the pane—
nothing but tears streaming,
nothing to say.

LAZARUS, ON HIS SECOND DEATHBED, REMEMBERS

At first I was horrified,

but there it was—a tingle
in the heavy ooze—something
I could feel like gravity
rotting on the slab,

a sudden shock of inhalation...recognition—
it was me—stench, heat, cold slime
on the move—worms in retreat maybe,
and a swarm—Bees? Flies? Bats? –
chitter-buzz-and-hum-all-at-once, sort of like
thoughts.

Then, bit by bit it all came back—the old geography—
inside-outside in the dark, the violent cresting arch
of backbone; then the seizure, the final rigor
reversing itself.

I never wanted this—
my throat on fire croaking
its new first word—*Again.*

BLOOD

No one knew just how it started. Maybe it was all the rain we'd had, then a single sunny day—an unaccustomed brilliance—saints in stained-glass making our eyes water and blur, or maybe it was a cloud drifting across the sun that made their robes seem to ripple in an unfelt breeze. Then somebody noticed Saint Patrick's right hand rise a little in benediction. Then all the statues began to move and cry as the tears and blood of a slaughtered god slickened his skin. Then the Virgin's blood, called forth from a deep well of agony, spilled down her robes.

Then everyone was happy—something sacred, at last, streaming into ordinary lives. Every single one of us was special, even crazy George who opened a vein and bled all over his sister's new dress. They took him off to the hospital, but everyone knew what he meant, what he wanted—that our blood too might mingle in the great myth, might flow forever in the echoes of its telling.

The Church sent out an expert to explain
how none of this was real—he was kind.
Nothing to worry about, he said. *This happens
all the time.*

    So, nobody was crazy, nobody blessed, no miracle.

Actually, I was away at school when all this happened. I took the first train home, but when I got off, folks had already started to forget. One of the excitable cousins told how, by the end, gods and saints and people were mingling, crying together for all the suffering the world had ever known—how they embraced, how they stained each other.

MATTHEW GANDALF

(June 23, 1969 to June 24, 1969)

You see, at the time I had this project...
I was building a world out of icicles
so I couldn't afford a mistake.

You hurtled in through a window
I didn't know was open,
and for a few hours

I handled you like a live grenade.
Then you did the only thing you could—
exploded from this world

faster than you entered it.
We hardly had time to give you a gift,
and then it was just some names,

an evangelist and a magician--
we threw them after you into the void.
I hope you can use them.

VALEDICTORY
For Gael Mathews (1955-1991)

She said:

When I die a hole will grow in your imagination.
It will take the shape of my form.
The dreamer will try to make good
what is missing.
He will do his best.

But this wound, it is a tender thing.
Raw winds will howl through your stomach.
I won't minimize the pain.
I won't dramatize it either.

Make of mourning a full-time job,
grief just another force of nature:
wind, glacier, desert, sea.
You will love it sometimes.
It will take the shape of my form.

Tears will come.
They will change as seasons change.

Your stake in this is the fullness of your breath:
to breathe so that you glow,
to suck in the sweet, sweet air
'til deepdown muscles heat up from the inside
and others find themselves in your words.

Remember the small stuff—
lilacs framed in an empty window,
the dew in my hair as I stepped out of the shower

and how you snapped my picture.
You'll find this Nothing has many sides and depths.
You can explore them now.

It's safe.

    I'm almost

               gone.

OPENING NIGHT

You were gone.
I was alone.

TV on for hours, poems
scattered and stained
on the drain board,

and that bottle
of Wild Turkey
standing tall
and golden
on the bookshelf…

And so I gambled,
snatched up
some poems,
ran out the door
to the open mic
before I could change
my mind.

The room was filled
with strangers
who called themselves
poets. It was weird
until I stood up,
looked into their eyes
and read.

How to describe it—
the gratitude I feel
even after all this time—
I used to think
you had to explain
yourself

but those eyes
so open and unblinking
and the hush they made,
and the chance,

that my life too
might echo in
the music
of an evening…

THE POET AT 70

Strong enough in who he is at last,
he shoots out tendrils into every shade
of winter. He's found a stake, a stance,

an umbilical sunk down deep and wide
into what's left of his dead.
Supple, mute, he begins to sway

to every tune he's ever overheard,
shifting shape in mysteries that rule
the vast ferocity of wind. And all the misery

stored up in him 'til now, has a name
and a local address. Meanwhile,
the massive and indifferent marketplace

begins to play to his strength—ten thousand
hours of drinking coffee and telling himself
the truth as best he could. He's found

that flexing membrane between himself
and the Great Fall. He's become a doc
who heals himself, who knows himself so deep

that trajectories of resurrection become
routine, as bit by bit his body wakes,
startled and rippling, like yesterday

when that tiny ache at the base
of the glottis thawed after thirty years,
turned, introduced itself and did a mighty backflip

into memory—that pulsing cataract
muscling ever backwards and away
from the edge of his moment—

blind, hushed, utterly out of his depth.

ANTHEM

...and then that night in '69
Jack and I in the rusted out old Ford—
windows open, cruising up from Baltimore—
me with a pregnant woman somewhere,
him with a woman in the ground—
us, twisting the dial over and over,
hoping for a brave new song
and how it felt like a jackpot
when we found it

Hey Jude, don't be afraid

Tires on the tarmac hummed
and the pitch-black breeze
mellowed into easy breath
and prayer and the cab filled up
with moonless selves and the truckers'
headlights signaled us

take a sad song and make it better

at last, a line that we could live by—
real as the wind rushing around in our ears.
We were never ready for that chant
to end, for the night to shrink back
into static and silence—

remember to let her under your skin

We never guessed that nights like this
were the beginning of our history,
that poetry would come to us like this—
throbbing met by darkness on the move
in this, our fierce new labor...tuning in

AUTOBIOGRAPHY OF A STRANGER
(for Carlos Rodriguez)

I was a kid shivering on city busses
when I began to see myself
in the eyes of fellow riders—all of us

hunched and bumping at 6:AM or midnight.
And then, for no good reason, I began to talk to them
like you're not supposed to, saying a little more

than what's required by time or situation.
It was risky, yet so much seemed to depend on it—
the stakes were who I'd be and where.

I noticed when we talked, they seemed
a little less strangled, unheeded and given up on.
So I got courageous, spoke of last things, big things

from Philosophy class like what was worth
doing before the end, or how light has no form
but falls on everything alike and makes us possible

to one another. After a few weeks I stopped.
I don't know why. Maybe I lost my immunity
to embarrassment or got in trouble with somebody,

or maybe it was time to freeze
into a more abstract version of myself,
something the world could recognize

from a distance. So I began the work of settling in
to the common web of calculation. Yet at night
I dreamt of vast spaces in the weave,

built up that store of longing for a *thou*
to see me through the really dark days.
Now, that I am old, I once again say more

than what's expected in cramped spaces—
like on an elevator, maybe, where there's just time
for a tiny bit of excess, time to venture more

than what we say about the weather.

Jesus is my religion and pool is my game

…he said. And right away I knew I was in trouble…but wasn't that the story of my life…the wrong barstool at the wrong time. Then he rushed out without even chugging down his beer. I heard he went to a family wedding, exposed himself to the bride and then his uncle beat him up and threw him back into the VA, where he didn't take his meds. And then the VA threw him out and he came back to the bar. He said, *I need a beautiful friendship.* I said, *Why didn't you take your meds?* He said, *they make me crazy. I'd rather get beat up and thrown into the nuthouse than swallow that shit. So how about it—will you be my friend?* The truth was, I wanted to be dangerous like him, but I had two big holes inside me, and I didn't know their names— maybe *Jesus* and *Pool* would do. *Sure*, I said.

GRANDAD'S TRIP

When he was seventy, he drove all the way in
from California with a trunkfull

of marijuana. He'd heard
it was a cure for schizophrenia.

He drove through every kind of state.
Sometimes what he did was called a crime,

sometimes it wasn't. In some towns folks were wide awake.
In some they tossed and turned in bitter old trances.

He didn't care. All he wanted was to save someone he loved
from the hunger of her dreams.

The risk was nothing. He didn't think, he drove.
Once or twice a day he stopped for gas

and a sandwich. When he arrived in Philly
the stash was wilted, the cure of course—

an empty rumor. But that drive,
that endless drive, it changed him.

It changed him into what he'd do,
what he'd always do until the end,

for love.

AHKMATOVA'S TRIUMPH

In the awful years of the Yezhovian horror, I spent seventeen months standing in line in front of various prisons in Leningrad. One day someone "recognized" me. Then a woman with blue lips, who was standing behind me, and who, of course, had never heard my name, came out of the stupor which typified all of us, and whispered into my ear (everyone there spoke only in whispers):
   –Can you describe this?
   And I said:
   –I can.
   Then something like a fleeting smile passed over what had once been her face.

*

I wait.

A litter of pigeons at my ankles
pecks at stone—winter angels of the Neva.

Am I the last of our kind to remember
your face? Can you feel me through these prison walls—
how I wait with the others, hoping for word?

If you were dead, would I know it?
Would my agony summon you like it does this poem?
Would you pass like an angel through the stone of your
dungeon—spirit triumphant?

And if you were freed, would I know you?
Or would our twisted faces miss each other?

My feet hurt. I lean exhausted up against these walls—
ashamed of myself, how much I need them.

I am hardly who I was…poetess, lioness.
I need a thousand names for cruelty just to make it through a day,
a thousand more for gray light oozing through the afternoon.
Here, where everyone whispers, I keep my face the same as all the others.
I am one-who-waits.

How to describe all this—
long line of thin gray coats outside the Lubyanka
mute guards, deep cell, night-chill, you…

I burn whatever comes to hand for warmth—
all the old icons—cliché of my biography, useless memory
of your father—nothing left of me but body—
inexplicable rising heat, sucking lungs, tiny breaths
steaming in the smack of the cold—here, gone.

This is my triumph:

I breathe,
shift from one foot to the other, shiver
in the pigeon-gray light.

I endure.

I describe it all—
agony and breath, form and dissolution.

I cannot free you. Forgive me.

SENSEI

Just before I left for good, I said,
"You never taught me anything."
You gazed on me, gleaming,
with a look much stranger than love.
Amused at invisible ironies,
you shook your head. *Did you
really know what you were doing?
Did you know then what
it took me all these years to find?*

He was a demon. He was a gift—
my brooding nightmare incarnate
who left his scent,
cigar smoke in the elevator—
a warning to be ready,
when the doors opened.

We clutched at recipes. He mocked us.
We puffed ourselves with stale success.
He whirled, kicked, walked on
to something interesting.

We were like newborns—
slithering, shining, gasping—
squirming to fit in a spinning world.

He called us by our missing names—

Poet without a Tongue,
Bridegroom without a Bride,
Warrior without a Cause,
Witch, Scholar, Healer, Clown--
"*Use this, Use this*" he said.
"*Be! Be!*" he said
as he shook us at ourselves.

Through it all he whispered,

"Go deep into your *own* darkness
and you'll never be lost
in the madness of others."

He fought hard for everything
wild, fine, and dangerous in us.
One by one we stumbled forward,
finally learned to dare a bit—
men, women who stepped up
to their time, who shed the skin
of dead careers, to dream
of something grander:

to stand still in a hurricane,

to breathe in a vacuum,

to make of rage a tool
and not a master.

One by one we found
a dragon fighting next to us,
side by side, singing
in the golden air, breathing
in the dust of fallen kingdoms—

We
     know
          joy.
We know
     the bullet
          initialed just for us.
We push on,
     deeper into this breathing world,
          Blinking,
               Wounded,
                    Whole.

ODE TO THE ORDER

For the Brothers of the Christian Schools

I thought the beauty of the evening done
when the sun slipped out of sight.
I shrugged, turned again from everything
that couldn't be helped. But strong
fingers dug into my shoulders, held me still,
and I saw, for the first time,
a sun's lavender ghosts ripple
in a full swath of sky.

They were always doing stuff like that—
holding us still at crucial moments,
helping us to find a stance
in what was left of vanished things.
When they looked into our eyes
it was God they saw looking back at them—
clear and open.

But we sensed an absence
under those robes—that darkness
they took for uniform—something
alien, renounced—what was it?
In the end we could not find ourselves
in their invisibility, turned our backs,
stumbled out into our own raw lives.

> *I hated you for virtues*
> *that led me to forget the poor body*
> *that wants and wants but has no tongue.*
> *You didn't mind much, you weren't*
> *literal beings anyway; existence for you*
> *was your own kind of story, a strange mix*
> *of renunciation and urgency, a pilgrimage*
> *to an edge I couldn't see.*

When I got married, I made a bet with God.
Took all my chips and put them on a spot
marked "Human Flesh." I lost:
the bad years, the dying wife, the body
frozen into stone, the vanished knack of prayer...

They came to me then in dreams,
waved me on to follow,
showed me how to step
into their kind of mystery
breathing, eternal, buried
in the next second...

These days I keep slipping from the path—
soft temptations of heart and eye,
infinite gradations of gold and brown-
is it an artist's eye I have or a sinner's?
I mean, what do we really know of soul—

endangered species crawling under rocks,
alien courage sniffing for a sign
to remind it of itself...

They asked me to join them once.
I threw up all over their shoes.
They were gentle, smiled, granted me
my wretchedness. Now that it's too late

I wonder-- *if I had chased after*
your pristine surety, what then?
Would I be allowed to pray
in the old way--
wanton, unreserved?

NUNS

They took their names from the myths they lived.
Jane, Sally and Marge became

Sister Irene Joseph

Sister Michael Francis

Sister Joseph de Lourdes.

In robes of great mystery they strode like queens
through the hallways of our school.

On the left hand they wore a gold band.
They were brides of Christ.

We were their children.
They mothered us.
We wore them out.

But sometimes it took fifty years
in a class with fifty boys.

The ancient ones were glad to sacrifice
themselves—to suffer like the Christ suffered,

to get ever closer to that agony,
to take it into their bodies.

I still don't understand them.

They were the strongest women I knew.

TYGER, TYGER

Because I do not want a life that's numb,
I crawl out on my belly to an edge where I'm not anymore
me—just a dumb jumble of pressure, itch and image
seething in the seismic ground of everything
ignored, missed
while He—
fierce, indifferent, burning—waits
hidden in dense tapestries of dream and muscle
where I am a stranger to myself
and he is texture-on-the-move,
breath-paced flexing in the weave.

This ground we fight for isn't much—
just the space this body takes and the little one beyond
it warms up into; and though we know next to nothing
about each other, I know that this afternoon
he'll pounce. I watch how he sits
up and to the right, engulfed in an embroidery of leaves,
quickening
to the struggle, to how I'll taste, to how I'll feel sliding down
into the steamy blood-soaked center—blinded, broken,
dissolved
into his heat.

I'm trying to remember what I learned yesterday
about the mind—how meat shredded away from bone,
how juices given up, can feed a greater strength;
how I am not completely lost by evening,
just pared down, mobile. I can go anywhere
inside him then, but I like the space behind his eyes the best,
where I can see the world as he does, noiseless
but for what the shining needs—breath, pulse,
a kind of hum.

UNDERWORLD

He who has forgotten how to shine
examines his intestines as truly as he can—

gurgle, cramp, convulsing pit of snakes, he says.

He hears a rumor that he's really made of lightning—
a mighty flash unmeasured by the darkness of his time,

but when he looks at commuters on the platform
he sees instead of skin, a sheen of chitin,
fresh bulge of antennae, mindless chomping mandibles.
He hears the buzz of a frantic hive
where dirges ought to be. He longs to weep alone
for something lost and overgrown,
to feel a fresh self rise, dripping,
from a thousand years of roots and rain and silence.

He needs
something like a god to keep him company—
a daily resurrection to believe in,
a sweep of earth and sky
to breathe without a doubt.   He says Jesus—
and a white man with a chestnut beard appears—
Byzantine middle-class youth, exquisitely coiffed,
who knows more than he is saying…

> *What ever happened to you, in the desert—*
> *the tangled, matted hair, the days of eating bugs*
> *and drinking any liquid you could find?*
> *What happened to the danger you grew into—*
> *the blossom lopped, the roots entangling deep?*
> *I want to feel it—the underworld doing its job—*
> *seeds, roots, futures hatching everywhere.*

He feels like meat-for-chopping. He wants
to mean again. So he leaves his old friend
hanging on the cross and calls out other names—
Buddha is more jolly,
    Poseidon more wet,
        Yaweh more bloody-and-gone,
            Allah more alive in an ornate madness…

So he moves out beyond them to an edge
where it's not the pit of hell he sees but a wild savannah
where a thousand-mile breeze blows on and on
without intention, howling through the groan and pulse
of soul consuming soul. Nothing here but an old ferocity
wanting its truth back, its balance, its vastness, its indifference,
its mysterious shifting gravities. It wants its name. It wants him as he is—

    tiny, abject

        like a root

            like a seed.

GRANDFATHER PLAYS CHESS WITH DEATH

He watches, rapt.

The hooded master never stops
moving its pieces.

The proud old man
never even moves a single pawn.

The manic skeleton clicks and clacks
its mandible in glee…

and maybe for the final time, Pop takes up
the work he loves--that zest

to pierce to the pulsing root of daydream,
to ease into the body's web of tension,

hush its chatter, breathe its breath,
follow every wince and blink

into all that's next.
The bony finger jabs

from a draping sleeve
and slowly rises.

He stares back, steady as a mirror.

When his king is tipped and the monster
sweeps the board, he does not avert his eyes.

The death-head's empty sockets suck him in.
He waits there in the dark for an echo of his own great voice—

those eyes, those lethal, empty eyes are merely dreams.
Whose eyes? Whose dreams?

He grins and sets his king back on its square.

AT THE AT&T STOCKHOLDERS MEETING, OCTOBER 31, 1970

...and there I was—surrounded by my friends—all decked out in my purple top hat, yellow feather, sky blue sport coat and clown mask with a big red nose. It didn't bother us a bit that we were outside looking in, or that the cops were out in force. Some of us lobbed firecrackers at the fat cats on the sidewalk. They sounded like gunshots. We wanted to wake them up. We wanted them to feel like Vietnam. And I was on the move at the center of it all. Friends clustered around me, fireworks at the ready. The cops on their horses waded into us and we scattered. But everyone knew to look for the top-hat towering in the crowd. We regrouped and started acting up again. It was a marvelous game. We almost forgot about Vietnam. At the end of the day, we faced a row of massive horses. The cops looked hot and nasty. The horses looked into our eyes. Someone lobbed a firecracker. They charged. We ran like the wind. It was thrilling, like in a Russian novel. I ditched the jacket and the mask in a dumpster. I kept the hat.

CONFIDENCE

What is really lost when a civilization wearies and grows small is ...CONFIDENCE... confidence in the society in which one lives, belief in its philosophy, belief in its laws, and confidence in one's own mental powers. Vigor, energy, vitality—all great civilizations, or great civilizing epochs have had this weight of energy behind them.

> Kenneth Clark,
> *Civilization*

Our talk has sickened. We are lost.
See how the script breaks up –
Alpha, Omega and the rest

scatter to the winds,
no longer call to one another.
And those old straight lines that took

us home at dusk—nothing more
than dreams of an old road. And yet
what we see here, what we make

of what we see, secures in us
the one thing after another
we were born to. And what we plainly

hear—night huffing and puffing
in the pines, a giant singing
a giant's song—nestles our sleep.

Yes, what we see, what we hear,
and the molten supple mass it makes
of us—bubbling, thickening, cooling

into soul-before-speech—is suffused
in us so deep and so fantastical,
that centuries themselves seem

but simple tunes in our great opera.
Here, now—we…press…on…
our gaudy, mute and easy self

hums and huffs and howls
its body into shadow,
its dying into song.

WHY I DON'T MARCH ON THE 4TH OF JULY

*May I never learn to scorn
the body out of chaos born
to woman and to man.*

       Leonard Cohen

I don't need to sing of independence
but of connection and good luck.
I sing instead the epic
of our being here—the geography,
biology, the myth of it—the luck
that's lasted through wars, hurricanes,
quaking earth and plagues.

Strange how little you know of it—
the story that led up to you…
how far back it goes—
to that history of gestation—
twenty years brewing
in the dreams of a young girl—

before birth, before conception
to a name slotted into the cast
of a play that would have a thousand acts.

And before that—
ten thousand years
of lucky accidents
that led up to a night—
a key turning in the lock between
existence and nothing,
and there you were,
a pulsing scrap
showing up unreckoned
in the lush buzz of a family
in the middle of its myth.

So, that is why I will not leave
this tiny self for dead
on the parade ground
where we rehearse
heroic images of ourselves;

will not repeat the lies
that I have overheard—
that we are hard as rocks—
immortal, independent, invincible.

I will not clench my eyes,
blame the pain on others
or whatever comes to hand.

I'll not forget to bless my luck—
this thriving, this gift—

I'll remember how she held me close
clinging to the heartbeat
I'd never been without,
the one that thundered
in the great cave of her womb,
that was the base note of my taking shape,
that echoes even now in the world
that throbs against me.

NAMING DAY
(For Mireille[1])

We come today to celebrate a seed—
a speck primed to sprout and branch
out toward a dazzling horizon
that will be a human world.

This morning

we gather to bestow
the most persistent thing about you—
the first of many ornaments
through which you'll shine from a distance,
and through this whisp, this word,
the thread of your significance will spin
into the grand tapestry of other lives.

Now,

as we say your fragile name,
our warm thick breath thins out
into objectivity of mere air.
Yet by this word we fix you in a web
of speech and prayer that stretches
back past everything we name,
rippling in a more than human breeze—
ancestral, abundant, anonymous.

In the end we will ease
into nothing more than what we've been to you:

slender memory,

      ancient trance,

           invisible atmosphere

---

[1] Mirelle: A Hebrew name meaning "God spoke."

from which you'll draw a lifetime's breath—
effortless, like we do now—planted here,
at home in an immensity of cold morning,
receding into all that moves away from us.

What shall we call it—
universe, night we cannot let alone?

We, who paint the sky
with autobiography,
we offer it to you—connect the dots
between the stars even as they burst
into forever, faster than naming,
faster than breath.

Where we come from, where we go,
there are no names. We shiver here,
huddled around our magic,
we note the moments—

early winter sky on the move,
cutting wind, some water,
a little blood sometimes—

we, who are halfway to history,
want to be forgotten gently.
So, softly, softly we call you to us

    Mireille

On this day, November 25, 2001
Let it be put down that we

    stopped,
                stood still.

SURF MUSIC

Crackling bonfires burn for us up and down the beach—
strange blazing tongues flex and stretch up toward
an infinite indifference that kills them at the height
of their telling. What are they trying to say?

Out there, words turn foreign and fantastic:
black holes, anti-matter, a universe running
away from itself. When is a light year? Where?
Words break like dried sticks against this immensity,
and we can't think our way to space
where spark snaps into darkness.

Down here our fire's burned out almost. We stare
at how the coals contain their flames—
flickering, liquid, shifting, shadowed—
embers holding fast to what consumes them.

In a breath from out of midnight, this fierce union
of death and beauty flares to lick the faces
of the future—sons and daughters of my hosts—
doe-eyed, dumb as oxen around their parents
but dry kindling for starlight.

Like an old grandpa I wrap myself in sweats and blankets,
grow still and fantastic, begin my wearing away
into a hollow self—empty, happy, echoing all that's lost
and unremembered as constellations careen overhead
and eternal codes older than dreaming explode out
to the edge of here, where imagination gutters into night.

These sons and daughters—soon they'll slip away
from us into the muscular current of their own stories;
even now they wander into shadowed surf
where gods breathe just out of earshot
and lifetimes explode into myth—molten, drifting
faster than time.

Is this what living is?

Tinderbox bodies, starlight's transit, conflagrations
fed with whatever comes to hand?
Is this what dying is?

And to *know* all this in a lucky moment!
Time, space, mythos rippling just beyond will…
It is so still out here!
It is so still out here!

MUSE AT THE WEDDING
(For Michael and Lisa)

Two wild rivers collide and shoot
down a canyon, a rumpus

of white water moving at the speed
of destiny to a vast conclusion.

You can do this.
Make life up as you go along,

fly out to the end of it, look back,
sing the beauty of the world's

ten thousand things. Make it up. Know
your world as a place of magic. Learn

its laws, watch each other breathe, feel
your shape worn into, smooth or rough,

from a life in the light
of one another's' eye. Accept

the body's need for the myth of its death,
that sacrament—mere matter blessed

by attention taking shape
in crickets' August crescendo

or in the pulsing of a blood red heart, steaming
in the utter silence of a snowfall. Make it up.

It's said the Creator doesn't make one of anything,
makes millions of wildflowers, stars and

how many songs do you suppose there are?
How many poems? How many

still unwritten, waiting to wake up
and live by their wits, so many

open channels to the heart of human feeling,
this profusion, this abundance—I can't wish

too much, can't say enough. Make it up.
Take your heat and shine.

Make a limber life, a sharp divorce from
the old trance of one thing after another,

a glorious jailbreak from the cage of rage and grief.
Make it up. Follow the soul of your union,

its meandering search for a thousand names
for God writ large across the night sky.

Make it up.

BIOGRAPHY

Bill Van Buskirk has been a meter reader, model, professional gambler, management consultant, a Buddhist, a construction worker, community organizer, drug counselor, pacifist, university professor and step-father. Most of these adventures have found their way into his poems, which he loves to send out for publication. Sometimes they are accepted which makes him feel *really* good—like the whole world loves him. Most times they aren't. He has two books of poetry: *Everything that's Fragile is Important* and *This Wild Joy that Thrills Outside the Law*. He believes that poetry can be a kind of magic-in-language that captures energies that hum and shine outside our day jobs—like humor, awe, hope, gratitude, wonder, mournfulness, wisdom, memory, ghosts, stillness and silence. When he was ten, a nun told him he was born on Shakespeare's birthday. When he was eighteen he took a vow to never be bored again (That one got him into a lot of trouble.) He's been married three times: one annulment, one death, one divorce. When he was nineteen he decided to talk to everybody about important things. He made a lot of friends on the bus to school. But people started looking at him funny so he stopped. He learned a little bit about violence on the street. It wasn't for him. When he was twenty he found out who Shakespeare was. He was impressed. When he was twenty-three, he had a little son who died after one day on earth. When he was thirty, he decided he needed a career. He doesn't remember much of what happened after that.

Made in the USA
Middletown, DE
07 March 2023

26284250R00040